FORCES IN MOTION

THIS WAY AND THAT WAY

by Spencer Brinker

Consultant: Beth Gambro
Reading Specialist, Yorkville, Illinois

Minneapolis, Minnesota

Teaching Tips

Before Reading

- Look at the cover of the book. Discuss the picture and the title.
- Ask readers to brainstorm a list of what they already know about what makes moving things change direction. What can they expect to see in this book?
- Go on a picture walk, looking through the pictures to discuss vocabulary and make predictions about the text.

During Reading

- Read for purpose. Encourage readers to think about when things change directions in their own lives as they are reading.
- Ask readers to look for the details of the book. What are they learning about movement and changing directions?
- If readers encounter an unknown word, ask them to look at the sounds in the word. Then, ask them to look at the rest of the page. Are there any clues to help them understand?

After Reading

- Encourage readers to pick a buddy and reread the book together.
- Ask readers to name three examples from this book about when moving things change directions. Go back and find the pages that tell about these things.
- Ask readers to write or draw something they learned about motion and direction.

Credits: Cover and title page, © Jaren Jai Wicklund/Shutterstock; 3, © scanrail/iStock; 4, © AJ_Watt/iStock; 6,7, © FocusStocker/Shutterstock; 8,9, © Smileus/iStock; 10,11, © razihusin/Alamy; 13, © Jupiterimages/Getty; 14, © xpixel/Shutterstock; 15, © Sergey Novikov/Shutterstock; 16, © 5 second Studio/Shutterstock; 17, © RyanJLane/iStock; 18,19, © Tomsickova Tatyana/Shutterstock; 20,21, © wundervisuals/iStock; 22, © tonito84/iStock; 23TL, © anek.soowannaphoom/Shutterstock; 23TR, © michaelstephan-fotografie/Shutterstock; 23BL, © Pressmaster/Shutterstock; 23BM, © nexus 7/Shutterstock; 23BR, © Corepics VOF/Shutterstock.

Library of Congress Cataloging-in-Publication Data is available at www.loc.gov or upon request from the publisher.

ISBN: 978-1-63691-413-8 (hardcover)
ISBN: 978-1-63691-418-3 (paperback)
ISBN: 978-1-63691-423-7 (ebook)

Copyright © 2022 Bearport Publishing Company. All rights reserved. No part of this publication may be reproduced in whole or in part, stored in any retrieval system, or transmitted in any form or by any means, electronic, mechanical, photocopying, recording, or otherwise, without written permission from the publisher.

For more information, write to Bearport Publishing, 5357 Penn Avenue South, Minneapolis, MN 55419. Printed in the United States of America.

Contents

A Change in Motion............ 4

Moving This Way and That............... 22

Glossary 23

Index 24

Read More 24

Learn More Online...................... 24

About the Author 24

A Change in Motion

I love to play soccer.

The ball rolls to my friend.

She kicks it.

Smack!

What happens to its **motion**?

Motion is movement.

The ball rolls one way.

Then, kicking it makes it change **direction**.

Now, the ball goes another way.

Why does this happen?

A kick has **force**.

It can make the ball do something.

The force pushes the ball in a new direction.

A throwing force makes a baseball fly through the air.

Then, a player hits the ball with a bat.

The hitting force makes the ball change direction.

Sometimes, things change direction quickly.

Look at the flag.

It moves from side to side.

The flag waves with a pushing and pulling force.

Two people play ping-pong.

They hit the ball back and forth.

A lot of forces move the ball during the game.

Some forces are big.

They have a lot of **energy**.

My dog sees a cat.

He pulls with a lot of energy.

My dog is strong!

Other forces do not have much energy.

This boat is slow.

The wind makes it go.

But today the wind does not have much force.

There are forces making motion all around.

They send things this way and that way.

What forces do you see?

Moving This Way and That

A force can move from one thing to another thing.

A **pool** stick hits the white ball. This moves the ball.

Then, the white ball hits another ball. This force makes the other ball go!

22

Glossary

direction the path on which something is moving

energy a measure of how much work something can do

force a push or pull that makes things move

motion the act or process of changing place or position

pool a game where people use sticks to move balls

23

Index

change 4, 6, 10, 12
direction 6, 9–10, 12
energy 16, 18
motion 4, 6, 20
movement 6
pull 12, 16
push 9, 12

Read More

Enz, Tammy. *Discover Forces (Discover Physical Science).* North Mankato, MN: Pebble, 2020.

Enz, Tammy. *Discover Motion (Discover Physical Science).* North Mankato, MN: Pebble, 2021.

Learn More Online

1. Go to **www.factsurfer.com** or scan the QR code below.
2. Enter "**This Way That Way**" into the search box.
3. Click on the cover of this book to see a list of websites.

About the Author

Spencer Brinker lives in Minnesota with his family. When they walk their dog, Linzer, they never know if he'll run this way or that!